Digital CRM: Strategies and Emerging Trends

Building Customer Relationship in the Digital Era

Marco Bardicchia

Table of Contents

CHAPTER 3: SEGMENTATION AND CONTENT PERSONALIZATION

Segmentation
- *What is market segmentation?*
- *Why segment the market?*
- *Demographic segmentation*
- *Psychographic segmentation*
- *Behavioral segmentation*
- *Geographic segmentation*
- *Using market segmentation*

Content Personalization
- *Content personalization by segmentation*
- *Persona-based personalization*
- *Customer journey-based personalization*
- *Individual-specific personalization*

Choosing the Method that's Right for You

CHAPTER 4: CUSTOMER VALUE MANAGEMENT

- Defining Customer Value Management
- The Benefits of Customer Value Management
- Using Customer Value Management
- Calculating Customer Value
- Changing Customer Value

CHAPTER 5: ANALYTICS AND PERFORMANCE MEASUREMENT

- Customer Retention
- Visits and Orders per Customer
- Sales
- Cross-Sells and Up-Sells
- Renewal Rates
- Sales Calls
- Winbacks Strategies
- Referrals
- Revenue per Salesperson
- Marketing Return on Investment
- Customer Lifetime Value
- CRM Metrics

CONCLUSION

Introduction

The world of today is vastly different from the one that people lived in even 10 or 20 years ago. As a whole, we focus on the digital more than the personal. We shop online. We buy things without ever having to touch them in person. We go out and work from the comfort of our home, thanks to the internet. This does not happen automatically; as the world has changed, businesses have had to evolve as well. Marketing has changed dramatically and is far different than what it once looked like.

One rule has held true; however: the customer is king. We must have relationships with our customers if we want to get those loyal repeat customers that drive our business. Customer centricity is essential. We have left behind the idea that we can just put up good ads and hope those campaigns can bring us the revenue that we want; we have to set up the right relationship with the customer to entice them to want to spend their money with us. We have to focus on the customer relationship so that we can know that we are on the right track.

Within this book, we are going to be addressing this fact. We are going to be analyzing the idea of Customer Relationship Management and discussing the ways that we can work to create it ourselves. We are going to consider all sorts of different strategies that you can use to help your own business begin to create that customer service mindset that you will need if you want to thrive. It is not as hard as many people realize to get started and get moving toward a customer relationship-oriented business model and marketing that will help you and CRM is the best way to make it happen.

When you know what you are doing, you can make sure that you have complete visibility over the data that you are going to be reliant upon to make sure that you are interacting with your customers the right way. It is effectively a model and program that you can use to do everything all at once. We will be looking at everything that you can do to make sure that ultimately, your CRM, your system, is working the way that it should for you and go into why it matters so much to your system. As you read, you will be introduced to digital CRM and the strategies that make it powerful. You will learn all about both segmentation and content personalization as just two of the methods that you can use to understand your company's efforts and marketing to make it as effective as possible.

Now, before we begin and get into the details, let's stop and take a look at a few key points. We need to discuss what Customer Relationship Management itself is, including its typical implementation scenario, and we need to talk about the history of Customer Relationship Management and how it has gone from what it used to be to what we now recognize today.

Defining Customer Relationship Management

Customer Relationship Management is one of many different approaches that allow for a company to manage and analyze its own interactions with customers—past, current, and potential. It makes heavy use of data analysis to take a close look at the history the customers that are being scoped out have with the company and then focuses on how to improve the relationships that exist by focusing on customer retention.

The alternative to focusing on customer retention would be focusing on getting as many sales as possible regardless of the outcome surrounding them, and that is not always the most effective approach to take. Think of it this way—if you have 100 people that you are marketing to, would you rather get 10 of them that are loyal and will be lifetime customers, or would you rather sell to all of them at least once, only to lose their business for some reason or another? Usually, getting fewer customers but keeping them around for longer is better than just getting a whole bunch of them that you poorly manage who decide that your company is not worth their time.

CRM, then, seeks to boost that relationship and elevate the interactions that you will have. It will allow you to streamline the processes that go into your customer interactions and help you to improve the profit margins while making sure that you maintain those solid relationships with those who truly matter to your business— the people.

CRM helps just about every team in a business run effectively. From sales to marketing, from customer service to development teams, being able to manage those interactions in one place means that the customers get the most streamlined relationship with the company possible. Of course, focusing on that relationship means that it gets better and better, and the customer feels more and more justified in remaining loyal to that company.

Typically, CRM has several key components that matter for it. They allow for building and managing relationships with customers through the use of several tactics that allow for an analysis of the interaction. When you take a look at CRM tools, you will see all sorts of different ways that you will be able to connect to your customers, from being able to market to identify sales campaigns.

The elements of CRM include:

- **Human resource management:** This is the usage of human resource and skills in various contexts throughout the organization in an effective manner. This is essential for an organization to help with the employees, the most important asset within the entire system. It aids in creating solid people strategy and analysis to foster growth and development.
- **Customer service:** This allows for the collection of customer information and purchasing patterns, collecting up all of the relevant information and then sharing it where it matters the most. This keeps everything in order so that anyone can help the individual at any point in time.
- **Salesforce automation:** This is a program that is designed to be used by the sales force of your team that allows for forecasting of sales, as well as recording the sales that are done, allowing for the potential interactions in the future to be predicted.
- **Lead management:** This allows you to look at the leads of sales and their distribution. It is typically utilized in various aspects of a business, from sales to marketing and customer service departments.
- **Marketing:** Making use of CRM allows for the assistance of marketing processes through

facilitating the effectiveness of strategies that you use. It typically encompasses elements such as campaign management or document management and will allow for the creation and enhancement of those marketing strategies that matter the most.

- **Workflow automation:** CRM works to automate the essential processes in hopes of creating something that is overall much more efficient than anything else. It allows for expenditure to be reduced due to the fact that it also works to eliminate the repetition of tasks.
- **Analytics:** This is used to analyze and present all data that is collected, allowing for it to be interpreted. It allows for the creation of histograms and other graphics that will help you to see current and past data to identify any trends.
- **Reporting:** CRMs work to allow for reports to be generated regularly, allowing for several different types to be generated, and it can aid in the forecasting of potential data that may be collected.

History of Customer Relationship Management

Despite what you may think, Customer Relationship Management is not something new—in fact, it is an ancient practice, one that we have, as a species, used for ages. Before we had currency to exchange with each other, we had trades. The first example that we are aware of trades occurring, as documented, occurred 20,000 years ago in what is now Papua New Guinea—knives made from obsidian were traded between islands. Some of the islands had obsidian, while others did not, and they worked to be able to trade.

CRM is effectively just working to manage the relationship that you, the seller, have with your buyer. In order to have that, there are just three factors that matter:

- The buyers and sellers
- The location
- What is wanted

With those three factors, CRM can then occur. Especially in the days when trade across seas or across long distances in the wilderness came with major risks, it was imperative to have those repeat traders that are able to be relied on as sources of income or trade, and so those that were sent out to do trading had to be skilled at doing so.

Of course, with trade comes a need for accounting as well. You needed to be able to record who bought what and who had which debts to pay off if you want to be able to record your profits. Names and locations were the earliest databases, and likely, they were put through segmentation to determine which customers were more important than others. While our reference to this practice of expert customer service and relationships is modern, the concept behind it is far from it.

As humanity advanced, we got computers; this, of course, led to us being able to automate processes. Starting in the late 1950s, automation and computer usage increased and the focus went to maintain detailed records for financial firms, such as banks, stock exchanges, and other departments. By the 70s, as the cost for a computer continued to drop, even small businesses were able to get in on the computer, making good use of it.

As account keeping continued to grow, people recorded information about their clients so that they would be able to work with their clients to the best of their abilities. They recorded the details of the interactions and sales, creating databases, and soon, it became commonplace to have digital databases filled up.

In the 1980s, we see a shift toward the modern CRM that we know today. Kate and Robert Kestnbaum created a form of marketing for databases in which direct marketing is analyzed against the customer database with statistics, allowing for the easy recognition of customers that are the most likely to make a purchase if approached and marketed toward. New concepts were created, new methodologies were implemented, and soon, we began to recognize ideas such as customer lifetime value and channel management.

In the 1990s, as these databases continued to grow and thrive, more products designed to aid in the management of customer data emerged. These products were a merge between database marketing and contact management, known as sales force automation. These products allowed for marketing to be optimized even further than before, and by the mid-90s, the market was even greater than before. The CRM systems that we have today were recognized as coming into existence.

In 1999, CRM made a shift, and we gained mobile and e-CRM by different companies, such as Siebel. It continued to grow further as well, with Salesforce creating a cloud system. Electronic and mobile CRM allowed for more devices and further uses, creating reliable and consistent products that would allow for quick usage. Likewise, the cloud service creation that Salesforce pushed was viewed as problematic in those earlier days; it was viewed as little more than a fad that would fade. However, their software as a service model ended up becoming one of the most popular, and Salesforce became the leading provider for CRM.

Nowadays, the market is continuing to expand. We still see new products released, and vendors often change to create alternative choices for different programming sets that people may want or need. Lately, there has been a shift to focusing on social data and just how important direct interaction with customers is when considering social platforms. It becomes imperative that we are able to look at the ways in which we interact with the people so that we can give them everything that we will need to provide them to keep them coming back for more.

This brings us to today, then, a time in which social media, the internet and so much more have made us more connected to our customers than ever. They can message us night or day, regardless of our hours, and we can get back to them. We can track their shopping and spending habits to provide them with recommendations that will keep them coming back for more over and over again and all we have to do is embrace the modern-day changes and the advent of the smartphone and mobile data.

Chapter 1: Digital Customer Relationship Management

As the world has changed, so too have our standards and what it is that we must do if we hope to stay afloat and ahead of the constantly changing standards that businesses are held to. The people have integrated with their technology—so now we need to do the same. The world has turned to their ability to connect constantly and we must follow with them. We must be able to make the necessary changes to stay relevant, and digital CRM is how we do that. We already have CRM capabilities—so moving one step forward toward a digital basis is not actually that outrageous of a shift to make.

Digital CRM, then, takes traditional CRM to a whole new level. Instead of seeing it as a tool, it is guidance for how we can create those long-term and sometimes even lifelong interactions that we want during the customer journey. We work to push the spotlight onto the ways that we can enhance the experience of our customers' interactions every time they find that they have to. Everything, from stepping into the store to checking out, to even leaving reviews or contacting online services for help, must be the most pleasant interaction it possibly can to ensure that the people *want* to come back.

Think about it—we have more competition than ever before these days. There is not a single type of product that you cannot find a replacement for. You may specialize in shoes and sell shoes with a specific marketing ploy, but if people decide that they do not actually like your marketing strategy, they have no shortage of other shoe sellers to shift to. Because there is rarely ever a true monopoly on products, there is no real way that you can force people to choose your product, whether they like it or not.

Because of this, we need CRM to guide our relationships with our customers. We need to be able to tailor our focus to those customers to try to foster loyalty so that we know that they are coming back, not because they *have* to, but because they *want* to. This is the key difference here; you must make sure that people love your company. When they do, they will naturally recommend you more and more and that will help you to get more business in the future as well. The customer becomes the end goal; the focus is not only that the customer is always right, but that the customer's experience can be enhanced to make the customer happy as well.

Within Digital CRM, you will get the structural foundation to allow for exactly that. You will be able to look at an inside out orientation in which you will be focusing on what you can do to interact with the customers, ensuring that they are as happy as they can be, and therefore granting you everything that you need to push forward. You are not just meeting customer expectations—you are exceeding them in hopes that your customer will be back again.

Digital Customer Relationship Management vs. Traditional Methods

CRM is used by companies to allow them to view and manage their data that pertains to their customers, but we know that customers today are changing. The vast majority of most people's markets make use of social networks and social media, and because of this, we need to make sure that we evolve. Traditional methods of CRM did not require as much interaction between people and companies to keep the products working effectively. There are some very key differences between the two that allows for the adaptation of traditional CRM into a digital landscape, and the sooner that transition is made, the sooner that companies are able to then fine-tune what they are doing with their customers to ensure that they get the results that they are looking for.

In digital CRM, your goal is not just sales—you are not just looking at that dollar sign above someone's profile. Rather, you are looking at the conversion of a customer along a journey. Sure, your customer may currently not be wealthy; perhaps, they are a student in college, but they go to your store to shop. One day, they may actually have the wealth that you want in a customer, but if you did not foster that relationship earlier on, you would find that you likely will lose them to someone that does care about their experience. Digital CRM cares about the journey into a regular customer that will then eventually translate to higher profits later on that are stabilized.

In particular, there are a few key ways in which digital CRM varies from traditional that are worth focusing on. First, let's consider the staff role. In a traditional CRM approach, everything that is done is dependent upon the data that then determines how to approach the customer. In digital CRM, however, the role is to make sure that quality is the key point driven between all content and all employees are able to access information about clients at any given time.

There are also different priorities of functionality; the traditional CRM system prefers to create workflows that are defaulted, and each and every stage is identical, regardless of the people that are being approached or their demographics. It is process-centric without really setting up any option for personalization to make sure that ultimately, everyone is getting what they need. Digital CRM, however, looks more at the way in which an individual's interactions with a particular business. It attempts to create a conversation-centric method rather than process-oriented; this allows for a more personalized, pleasant experience.

In terms of communication significance, traditional CRM has the company focusing on interacting with the people when it wants to. The company will put out ad campaigns or messages on its terms to connect with customers. It is more one-sided—there are not really any easy ways that lend themselves to direct feedback rapidly. With digital CRM, however, the focus is on creating that two-way dialogue. It is all about making sure that, ultimately, you are able to interact with others with ease. It is all about being able to sustain that engagement and listening to what people are saying. Think about how on social media these days, businesses are always calling for engagement—that is the end goal.

Ultimately, the processes in traditional CRM are all about sealing the deal—the end goal is simply getting through the transaction. You don't have to like each other with traditional CRM; the money just has to exchange hands. However, with digital RM, the relationships is king. Everything centers around the relationship between the company and the individual customers. They are deemed relevant, and it is deemed worthwhile to spend money trying to connect to the customers to make sure that they feel like their voices matter. After all, you cannot have a company if you do not have a client base.

The Importance of Digital CRM

Customers have expectations, and when we do not meet them, we do not get them to purchase from us again in the future. We must make sure that we are adhering to those customer expectations if we want to be successful. Ultimately, to meet customer expectations, we must:

- **Understand:** CRM will take a look at hurdles that are encountered from several different perspectives. We will be able to look from the management's role to address keeping everything functional and regulated, while we can also recognize that sometimes, we need to look from the customer's side as well. There is that leeway with CRM to ensure that just the right fit is tailored to the solution that the customer needs.
- **Develop:** CRM seeks to ensure that you are able to use a consistent method to ensure that you are measuring every customer's value, recognizing them as an individual, but also for the value that they bring. It is done through being able to provide the necessary analytical ability to understand the customer journey for each person.
- **Align:** The CRM model seeks to align a company's model with the customer journey together, weighing both of them and recognizing them as cross-functional to create a way in which everyone is working together toward the same goal in an agile manner.
- **Leverage:** We must be able to make the greatest use of data that we gather, and CRM allows us to leverage its technology to do just that. From tools to analytics as a foundation to discovering how to create generation and personalization, we are able to

get the whole picture, all wrapped up into just one package in a transparent manner that leaves everyone satisfied.

- **Integrate:** We must be able to ensure that there is the proper compliance to regulations, laws, and authorities and CRM allows for that as well, adding in the regulations for compliance into the programs itself.
- **Ensure:** CRM must ensure that we measure properly. It is imperative that companies must have an agile project team to ensure that resources are allocated to the best of their ability and value.

Digital CRM is highly relevant these days for those reasons. We have already been touching upon the ways in which digital CRM rules supreme above other options that exist. It is important due to the fact that the entire world has been shifting to something that is more digitally based. The entire world is working through social media and wants to be heard, and when you make your customers heard, you will find that they are much more likely to feel fulfilled and satisfied.

Ultimately, with digital CRM, the end goal is to ensure that customer satisfaction is achieved. This allows for an increase in the loyalty a customer feels and therefore makes them more likely to continue to use that particular company longer. They will be more likely to continue frequenting a business that they feel like is doing a good job, and that ultimately becomes the key here—getting those repeat shoppers or customers.

Digital CRM allows for that in particular, then. It makes the focus on gathering that necessary information that allows the company to discover those hidden patterns and that makes it highly important. When you know that Sally over there always buys products in certain quantities at certain times and you can begin to see that play out repeatedly, you can then take advantage of that information and begin to advertise those products heavily right around when you expected her to buy. This then ups your chances of success. Likewise, if you see that Susan is shopping around for pregnancy and ovulation tests, you can be pretty confident that she is trying to get pregnant—and, therefore, can begin to advertise heavily with baby gear.

It goes further than that; however, it goes to social media and watching how people interact with the posts of your company. You can see that they tend to be more responsive with very specific kinds of posts on your social media page, which may be tied to their shopping profile as well. You can then push those objects as well, and you can predict which other objects are going to draw attention.

The more you do this, the more the perceived quality of the products are. While it may seem strange to be tracking the habits of those that you are trying to sell to, it can actually go a long way in terms of making sure that the people that you are trying to market to actually feel appreciated and like you are paying attention. Even better, when they see products that are flagged as being something that they may like, they may even buy extra items instead of just the ones that they set out to purchase. This means that you may be able to up your sales as well.

Upping that client engagement, making it clear that your relationships with your client are more than one way at any given point in time, is highly important; it helps with retention as well and that eventually translates to responsiveness and easy problem solving that you are able to use to ensure that even when something goes wrong, your client or customer still feels important.

The Benefits of Digital CRM

There is a myriad of benefits to the use of digital CRM and marketing strategies that will help significantly with your numbers. Studies have shown that making sure that you focus on the customer relationship over anything else, numbers across the board are better. In particular, it has been cited that it costs between 4 and 10 times more to get a new client than it does to keep an older client around to repeat their transactions in the future. With that math, wouldn't you rather have a loyal client that wants to continue purchasing from you than trying to get new customers to replace them? There are a few particular stats that have been noted with the use of CRM strategies to create happy customers and therefore recurring profit margins. These include:

- Higher Conversion Rates
- Higher cross-sell and up-sell revenues
- Better customer winback rates
- Higher Customer Lifetime Value
- Higher revenues from customer referrals

Effectively, you are able to facilitate your relationship with your customer in just the right ways that you are able to maximize margins and ultimately have a more successful business model. These include:

- **Establishing visibility:** You are able to push your products, your company, and your services in the limelight with digital marketing thanks to the fact that you are reaching out to your customers; you are not passively placing ads in places and hoping that they will work. Rather, you are working to ensure that customers see that you are there by working to entice them to buy from you. Your company educates those potential buyers and works to convert prospects by making sure that it is aware of the most important details that it needs. It takes a look at personalizing content and conversations to make sure that their messages are heard as loudly as possible.

- **Enabling employees:** With a CRM program, all information about a client can be filed away so that when there is an interaction between the company and the client or customer, anything pertinent pulls up. You will be able to see social media engagement with the individual customer, as well as keywords that they tend to use and more. You will be able to tell what their recent purchases were and information about their spending habits. All of this helps the employees of a company to figure out exactly how to best approach the individual so that they can give them exactly what they need. This makes the marketer's job easier than ever, and in doing so, the customer also feels like they are getting that personalized service that they want.

- **Execute flawlessly:** This benefit of CRM programs allows for the information that is needed to ensure that ads and other outreach attempts are tailored specifically to the individual that is being approached at that point in time. It involves latching on to those key performance metrics to allow for a data-driven approach to the entire relationship with the customer. You will be able to see what they want and you can deliver.

- **Manage long-term goals:** CRM allows for all of the necessary data and analytics to be produced so that you are able to track all of your important goals and ensure that ultimately, the right kind of progress is being made so that those goals are met accordingly.

Chapter 2: Digital Customer Relationship Management Strategies

To have a successful business with CRM, CRM strategy is a must. You must ensure that you are able to balance the goals of a business to the customer expectations, and to do that, you must have a proper strategy to ensure that everything remains in balance. That strategy allows for the determination to be made to discover the extent to which CRM can aid in the business objectives by prioritizing in a way that makes the most sense for those goals to be achieved. Through the use of vision and a solid mission plan, CRM strategies are able to aid in communicating and ensuring that objectives are shared.

In order to be successful, then, there are a few key disparities that must be avoided. These disparities can create a major disconnect between the relationship and the business goals, disrupting the entire process. You must make sure that you are able to avoid these disparities through the use of a well-planned out CRM campaign and with several different CRM strategies. Let's first take a look at those disparities to avoid to ensure that you can start off on the right foot. By cutting these out first, you can then shift your focus to how to create effective personalization, which then leads to a more satisfied customer after a successful interaction.

1. **Lack of overview or responsibilities:** The first key disparity to avoid is a lack of overview or responsibilities. This will help to avoid the problem of losing sight of the bigger picture. You are not just looking at a single sale that you are trying to make in one specific moment—you are looking for a relationship. Those go two ways—and if you are not careful, you can let your own focus on just one sale prevent you from landing others. Remember, you are focused on the whole journey, not just the one step that you are on. Customers are focused on the entire experience, from the item that they have purchased to the experience with it to how the buying process was, and also how any problems were solved if there were any. When your company is focused entirely on getting that sale rather than looking at the bigger picture, you will run into problems.

2. **Lack of guidance:** It could be that your company has struggled to make sure that their brand experience is not aligned to each interaction the way that they wish it was. It could be that they are not providing that specific vision that they have and as a direct result, they are losing those repeat customers. Companies must make sure that they are working with their interactions to help meet expectations of customers thoroughly while also understanding that their customers have very specific needs that are driving them so that they can be aligned.

3. **Lack of feedback:** When the interaction design is cut off too soon or is too short, it can lead to a lack of data. The first plan that you put out probably is not going to be the right one for you; they usually need to be tailored over time and because of that, you will need to be realistic and recognize that as customer expectations and the perception of a brand change, you must also make sure that you are updating the

ways that you get your feedback to ensure that ultimately, your organization gets the clearest picture. Without it, the information that you are getting is likely inaccurate.

So, then, if you must avoid those points, but you need a way that you are able to drive your company toward that successful CRM, you may be wondering what you have to do. There are ultimately many different answers to that, but to have consistently successful customer interactions, there are a few key points that you must meet. These will enable you to ensure that ultimately, you will be getting things right the first time. The three primary factors for success are:

- **Prioritizing the journey:** We will be going over the customer journey in just a moment—but they must be prioritized. Make sure that journeys are prioritized, even if that means that certain customers or clients are primarily held by specific team members to ensure that they get the best possible experience as you interact with them. Make sure that you keep everything into consideration and remember that the journey is ultimately the key to that customer relationship that you need.

- **CRM principles:** It is also important that, if you want to make sure that you have successful customer interactions, you are able to create brand consistency by ensuring that you understand how to address the needs of the customers, as well as their priorities to ensure that you are maintaining a relationship. Remember, customers have specific needs that must be met to keep them satisfied.

- **Trial and error mentality:** Finally, consider the trial and error mentality. Let's be real here—there is no way for you to know exactly what to do the first time. It is important for you to be willing to interact and experiment to ensure that you can understand the best practices that you can use to optimize for a target audience. This requires you to be willing to try something new, record the results, and then use them accordingly, adapting if necessary.

The Customer Journey

The customer journey is that journey from a prospective customer all the way to a loyal one, and it serves as the framework for what it is that you have set out to do if you are looking to use a CRM model to maintain relationships with your customers long-term. It aids in establishing those repeat customers. You are a consumer yourself of some items—think about it this way. Would you rather shop at the store that makes you feel like they genuinely care about what you need and want, or would you rather go to the one that does not care much about customer feedback? Most people will err on the side of wanting that better interaction with the store; they want to be treated well to ensure that ultimately, they do get what they wanted.

Unfortunately, of new businesses, 50% are clueless about the customer journey and just how integral it is if you want to up your profits. They do not pay attention to the complete experience that any customer actually has within their organization; rather, they ignore the intricacies and focus on the sale itself. Sound familiar? That was one of the ways to fail at integrating with a CRM and is one that must be avoided. Let's take a look at the steps of the customer journey, from awareness all the way to loyalty.

The customer journey can be divided into three general categories—before purchase, during purchase, and after purchase. Each of these is quite straightforward and serves their own purposes. Each of them also involves different approaches to the contact that is had with the individual. In particular, you can expect to see the following methods hold true:

Before purchase:

- Contact with social media
- Contact with ratings and reviews of products
- Testimonials
- Online advertising
- Word of mouth

During purchase:

- Visiting the store or office
- Visiting the website or viewing the catalog
- Viewing promotions on that item at that moment

After purchase:

- Billing
- Marketing emails
- Support teams or customer service
- Transactional emails

More specifically, however, you can expect to see seven key phases that a customer goes through during this timeline. You can expect to see customers go through these depending upon the guidance that you give them. They may go through a few steps on their own, but if you are not spot-on with your care and approach to the individual, you will find that ultimately, you will not see the interactions that lead to loyalty.

1. **A customer has a problem:** During this phase, the customer has a problem. They may need a product or something else that will help them. They are experiencing a situation that would cause them to require your product. Let's say that you sell silicone kitchen utensils that are designed to be used with Teflon pots and pans. The customer has just torn up another Teflon pan and is upset because their eggs are ruined for breakfast.

2. **A customer wants a solution:** With the problem in mind, the customer now thinks about what could happen to solve the problem. Perhaps he is looking at that metal spatula that he was given by a friend that only ever uses cast iron pans that are not damaged by steel, but his Teflon pans will not tolerate it. He thinks about what he could do to solve the problem. He could buy a new pan, obviously, but the same result will happen anyway. The next pan will be just as torn up as the last one because all he has is the metal spatula.

3. **The customer discovers the product:** Next, the customer discovers a way that he can solve the problem in the future—he sees an ad for silicone spatulas, made by your company, while he is shopping around for a new pan that is not chipping. "Oh!" he realizes, "These silicone spatulas will not destroy my pan. Perfect!" So, he heads off to go buy it.

4. **Product is experienced:** So, your customer buys the pan and buys the item. He tries it out that night at home to see how well it works and if that was really a viable solution that he could use after all. Sure enough, it works!

5. **Problem is solved:** He continues to use the spatula for a while and discovers surprise! It works! He's happy—he knows that he can just use that new

spatula whenever he is hungry instead of relying on another one or changing his frying pan habits.

6. **Beneficial outcome:** He discovers that the spatula is reliable and over and over again, he continues to use it, realizing that ultimately, it was perfect for what he wanted to do. He realizes that he is highly satisfied with the way that it worked, and he decides that he needs more silicone utensils as well.

7. **Repeat customer:** With that beneficial outcome, he will likely be much more open to trying out more of those products in the future. He found that the product was so helpful that he really wants to make use of more of them. As he continues to buy more of your product, and he continues to enjoy them every time that he pulls them out, he realizes that he is thoroughly satisfied. If he is satisfied enough, he may even become a customer that is loyal for life.

Of course, if you want to really visualize the customer journey, one of the best ways to do so is with a map. With a customer journey map, you can have an excel sheet that will help you to write out and organize events, motivations, and struggles with this particular user's experience. The information then gets organized and output to create a visual to be able to view in the context of the business that you have.

The specific stages that you want to consider from your side, then, can be summarized as:

- **Awareness:** How did the other person discover your company? Was it via advertisements or through some other way? Perhaps word of mouth or seeing a post that someone else shared on social media? In the example earlier, the customer discovered the product, or became aware of it, through seeing the advertisement for them when shopping for pots and pans.

- **Consideration:** During this stage of the journey, the individual debates whether or not they should be using that product. This usually involves researching the one item and considering alternative choices to figure out which is the right one for the individual, and that will depend on all sorts of circumstances and will be largely unique.

- **Decision:** The customer then decides to make their choice and go to the store to purchase it, or orders it online for delivery for later.

- **Delivery and use:** The product is then provided for the individual to use. This stage could involve some customer service, or it could not, depending upon what the item is.

- **Loyalty and Advocacy:** Finally, the customer, if satisfied, decides to order again in the future, and also shares their experience with other people to let them know what they think about your product.

Lead Generation

Lead generation is the idea of identifying and cultivating any potential clients or customers to determine if they would be willing to buy your goods or services. Have you ever been cold-called by your insurance company, asking if you want to add life insurance to your policies? If so, your name probably ended up on a lead generation chart at some point, and they ended up calling you because their software told them to.

Lead generation, as annoying as it can sometimes be from the other side, is actually a great way for your company to identify the individuals that may buy from them so that they can then purchase the items that they want and you can keep the business that you need all at the same time. Let's walk through this process of understanding lead generation and just how essential it is to a good CRM strategy.

First, let's identify what a lead is—a lead is any individual who may be interested in your company or that you have identified as being someone that will be likely to buy at some point. Typically, they have to provide some sort of information to your company first; perhaps that insurance agent calls after you were shopping around for quotes to get a good price and entered your phone number to see what they were offering. They collect that information from you and then use it to contact you later on. You showed interest, even if just barely, and that is enough for them to identify you as a potential client. So, off they go, calling you at inopportune times.

Your leads are likely to come in one of four forms:

- **Marketing qualified lead:** These are contacts that have engaged with you before but are not quite ready to engage yet. It could be that they have entered their information in but have said that they will think about whether they actually want to make the purchase.
- **Sales qualified leads:** These are contacts that have taken actions that show that they are absolutely interested in becoming a customer. Perhaps it is someone that wants to buy a car and puts in the paperwork for a loan.
- **Product qualified lead:** These are contacts who have used your products before and have indicated that they may be interested in becoming a paid customer. Usually, these are people who used a

product trial and are interested in the features that are available only after payment.

- **Service qualified lead:** These are those who have indicated directly to your team that they want to become a customer. For example, they are people who have explicitly said that they would like to upgrade a subscription to the next level at that point in time.

When you are acting to generate leads, then you are trying to attract and convert prospects to get them interested in what you have to offer. Some of the most common examples that you may not have realized include coupons, blogs, online content, live marketing events, and even job applications, which ask for information from you. Notice how with all of those lead generation examples, it involves the other party, the potential lead, reaching out first. With inbound marketing, which CRM focuses on, you can see that the first contact is always established by the other party. They show that they are organically interested, and then you can make the transition from stranger to having that customer-provider relationship that much more naturally.

Generating leads is not particularly difficult. You just have to follow a few steps to get those other parties interested, and the vast majority of what you will see throughout the rest of this chapter could work as lead generation methods. The steps to generating a lead are:

1. The visitor discovers your company, business, or product through one of the ways that you are currently marketing or advertising, such as on your website, social media, or even an ad.
2. The visitor clicks on the call to action—the image or button that will then bring your visitor to action. This could be the add to cart button, or it could be

the button to request more information, depending upon the product and what it is that you intend to do.

3. Next, the call to action takes your visitor to what is known as a landing age—a webpage that is designed specifically for gathering that information in exchange for something else. They may simply buy at this point. It could be that you are asking for an email address for a free trial of your product or something similar.

4. In the landing page, your visitor then fills out whatever the form is in exchange to get what they wanted. This is perhaps the easiest way to get that lead generated in the most organic way possible.

Essentially, then, your visitor gives you their information in exchange for something else, whether it is a product, a quote, or anything. That exchange, that mutual transaction, becomes the foundation for the entire relationship, and from there, you are able to then pursue the leads in other ways.

Your leads are usually attracted through one of three primary means, depending upon the type of business or company that you are: It could have come from email marketing, social media in some way, or through a blog. Of course, there are other ways that you can get leads as well, such as through the use of search engine optimization so that your webpage comes up sooner than other ones when certain keywords are typed in. You could have other ways as well—you could have compelling ads on banners or anything else. When the lead is generated, you can then begin to make use of other strategies such as the ones that we are about to talk about to push further and close the deal.

Email Marketing

Email marketing is one of the greatest ways to reach out to those that already know you well enough to provide their email. Email, despite the fact that many younger people are starting to lose interest, is still alive and kicking, and many people prefer email to any other form of contact they would rather be emailed about a product that is being offered than have them approached in other ways. They would prefer to ensure that they get those emails with everything all nice and neatly in one place so that they can make their decision.

When you make contact via email, the lead had to have provided that email for you at some point, meaning that they were clearly interested enough in your products at some point; you just have to entice them to buy again. You can do this in all sorts of different ways, but there are a few keys to ensuring that your email marketing is effective.

If you have any doubts about how effective this would be, consider that a whopping 85% of the adult users on the internet in the United States make use of email, which is 15% more than people who regularly use search engines and 22% more than social media users—meaning that email is wildly effective if you can use it effectively.

Remember that your emails should be tailored to the readers; your email has to be compelling enough for people to open them up, or otherwise, you are going to find that your readers probably will never actually finish reading them. Your email needs to stand out, but be polite, and it needs to get to the point as quickly as possible—no one wants a massive wall of text that resembles a rambling blog post all just asking for something to be purchased or donated. Remember these keys if you want to ensure that your particular email campaign will be as effective as possible:

1. **Collect emails:** Of course, you need email addresses before you are able to send out email lists. Make sure that you do this by providing something of value to your customer first. Make it an exchange so that you both get something valuable out of it.

2. **Send targeted campaigns:** Next, you want to consider ensuring that you have email lists with different user segments. We will get to those segments later on. For now, keep in mind that you will want to ensure that you have several different types of emails at your disposal based on where in the journey your individual customers are. You should have, at minimum emails for:
   - Welcoming
   - Curating
   - Engaging
   - Referrals
   - Discount offers
   - Cart abandonment
   - Order confirmation
   - Upsell or cross-sell
   - Re-engagement
   - Surveys
   - Customer appreciation

3. **Make sure people want to open your emails:** You need to make sure that your email is as catchy and personalized as possible to get people to open them. The easiest way to do this is through recognizing general human psychology and using that to your advantage. You will want to consider the following within your email:

- Personalization of some sort (Include their name in the headline)
- Urgency and scarcity (Limited time only!)
- Authority
- Trigger curiosity (Ask a question or tell them not to peek inside)
- Utility (Offer a solution to a problem)
- Numbers (Percentage of discounts or something similar)
- Social proof (Talk about other people wanting to do what you want them to do)

4. **Make them compelling:** Write them effectively and make sure that the tone, pictures, and even your call to action are all readily available. In particular, consider making sure that your emails are all mobile-friendly. This is perhaps one of the easiest things that you can do that will help you to ensure that your emails will get more interest. Remember, people are usually on the go—make sure that you format your emails to those people who are on their phones.

Push Notifications

Push notification marketing is a strategy that is a bit different—you are able to create notifications on web browsers or on phones that are tailored to the individual in hopes that you will win them over somehow. Push notification marketing is common for just about any service; it works well to send either transactional notifications, such as the status of an order or promotional when you are advertising.

Push notifications are quite powerful because they are able to meet a few key roles and offer:

- Better outreach
- Insights to viewers
- Better security
- A cheap option for communication
- Higher levels of customer engagement

If you want to send push notifications, you have two key options: Mobile or browser notifications. They each have their place. Mobile notifications will send popup messages to the individual's phone or mobile device that will allow for sending all sorts of reminders and alerts. This typically requires the user to install your app to allow the app to then send notifications. With browser notifications, your user will be prompted to grant permission to receive notifications, and the marketer can then push those ads without an app or anything else. There are websites, such as SendPulse, that will allow for this process to happen.

Cart Abandonment Strategies

No one likes to see that they had someone adding items to the cart... and then abandoned it. However, it happens often; people add items as they window shop online, but then never pull the trigger and enter their payment information. It is estimated that right around 70% of carts online get abandoned, and as a result, sales are lost regularly. However, there are ways that you can prevent this. You can lose money to this in other ways as well—you may send follow up emails asking if they intend to come back or trying to entice them. You may have to offer extra discounts in hopes of bringing them back. However, these strategies can really aid in ensuring that you are not losing sales to abandoned carts:

- **Make your shipping free:** The number-one reason that people abandon their carts is due to the cost of shipping. If they see that the price of shipping is high and they did not know that before, they suddenly see their total price skyrocket when they shift over to their purchase page, and as a result, they decide to abandon it instead. You could offer free shipping at a minimum purchase amount or during specific timeframes or for those that specifically abandon their carts if you want to send them remarketing emails. If you do not want people to use free shipping, you can also encourage people to pay by offering an express shipping option at a specific price as well.
- **Offer a guest checkout:** People also abandon their shopping carts because they do not want to go through the account setup process. However, if you set up a guest offer and they realize that they do not have to set up the new account, you then let them skip the hassle. After they purchase, they will probably create an account anyway so that they can track their order.
- **Make checkout a breeze:** No one wants a checkout process that takes forever. It should be simple and preferably on one page, even if you have them in segments on the same page. Make sure that you make it clear what they are being asked to do and what will happen next, as well as offering an explanation for why you are asking for everything. Also, offer a back button to the site and an edit button as well so that they can get everything just right as they check out.
- **Apply coupons automatically:** It can help for customers to see that there are discounts that are auto-applied to their order; this makes them realize

that they are getting a discount of some sort and they will not leave the site looking for one, at which point, they may get distracted or never bother finishing up.

- **Offer live chat on your webpage:** Make sure that your customers always have an option to get to a live person if they need it simply, or at the very least, can send an email to get a quick response if at strange hours. Easy contact to aid in any problems can help people decide not to drop their products.

- **Have a solid return policy:** If you want to make sure that people do not decide to leave your site, make sure that returns are easier. Many people, in particular, will not purchase if they cannot return their items for free. There should be a deadline for returns, as well as make your return information readily available for the individual so that they are aware of it.

SMS

Similar to email marketing, using SMS to market is a great way to send out short and sweet messages, offering promotions that are going on right at that moment. They are perfect for time-sensitive offers, especially since most people have their phones on them more often than not. SMS is text messaging—it is simple and to the point. There are a few key practices that ought to be considered when making use of SMS marketing, however, including:

- **Ask permission:** Most countries require you to ask for permission before marketing to cell phones via SMS. Make sure they give you permission first.

- **Pay attention to time and time zones:** Make sure that you are also mindful of the time at which you send these messages. While emails rarely ever bother people when they are sent, you can run into problems if you were to text people at 1 or 2 in the morning—they probably will not care to use that coupon that woke them up.

- **Identify your company:** Make sure that when you are sending messages, you need to add your company's name into it—most bulk SMS are sent from shortcodes, meaning that you will have a short, 5 or 6 digit number that they view, and they will not know who you are if you do not tell them.
- **Make this complementary:** This is probably not going to be your main campaign path. Make sure that you are using it in tandem with other options as well.

Direct Mailing

Direct mailing allows you to market directly to your prospect's mailbox or door. This is commonly done especially right around the holidays; corporations typically send out a big ad for their holiday sales to try to build up hype. It is the physical equivalent to email marketing. However, some people still enjoy physical correspondence.

If you want to direct mail to people, you will only need to offer up information that shows your business's name, a call to action, and a way that you are able to be contacted. Everything else can be as unique as you want. Some prefer advertisements or catalogs. Others will send coupons or customized content. What you choose to send will depend greatly on the content that you care to provide.

Direct mail is actually able to get a higher rate of response than many other forms of contact, surprisingly enough. It is 5.3% higher than email's abysmal 0.6% response rate, and the reasons are actually quite straightforward when you think about it:

- **You can interact with direct mail:** Mail has to be collected from the mailbox and will then directly clutter up their shelves or table if they do not get rid of it—which requires them to open it up or look at it to determine if it is important or not. With emails, people can glance at the headline and decide to ignore it if it does not matter. If it is something in an envelope, however, you have to open and read it to determine what to do with it.
- **It reaches everyone:** When you send out direct mail, you can reach out to just about everyone. If you live in a house or apartment, you have a mailbox and because of that, you will probably be collecting mail. The elderly populations have no problems with physical mail, and the younger generations will also glance at it to determine what to do with it just out of necessity, meaning that you reach more people.
- **It is versatile:** There are almost no limits to physical mail—so long as it fits in an envelope, you can send it. Do you want a card that pops out as soon as you open it? Do you want to explode glitter? You might annoy a lot of people with that last one, but you can do it if you want to. You can do just about anything with your advertising campaigns, so long as they fit in an envelope. You are not limited to just what will fit with mobile screens.
- **It is losing favor:** You have so much less competition these days than before; many companies are preferring to shift to digital methods of marketing thanks to it being easier to manage, meaning that you have more of a chance of being noticed.

Onsite Activities

If you are trying to catch people online, you probably want to make use of some online-specific options for marketing in hopes of enticing people to sign up for something or even to buy something. You can actually boost your engagement significantly if you were to use onsite activities that are designed specifically to get people to stick around longer than before. All you have to do is be mindful of what it is that you are trying to do. In particular, we are going to take a look at preventing the exit banners, upselling, and cross-selling.

Prevent-the-exit banners

Prevent the exit banners and popups are little popups that prompt the individual to remain on your page. It is a sort of last-ditch effort to trying to keep someone around. Perhaps you have a visitor that has entered your site and scrolled around but then went up to exit the page in the corner of their browser. As they moved their cursor toward the X to close the page, your page would then be prompted with a message asking them to stay on the site or trying to entice them to stay. The catch here is that you want to make sure that you offer something of value to try to keep them there. It could be that you offer them 10% discount on their next purchase if they sign up. It could be that you offer them a free trial of something if they engage further. There are a few different types that are commonly used:

- **Make the visitor feel special:** Leave a message inviting the visitor to join an exclusive club by joining a mailing list
- **Offer a discount:** This is highly enticing for most people

- **Advertise the most popular product:** Show a picture and a link to view a new product that the viewer may not have actually seen
- **Invite to an event:** Offer the viewer access to a conference or even a local event, if applicable
- **Promote other content:** You could even try redirecting the visitor to another area of your site that they may have missed.

Upselling and Cross-selling

Upselling is the act of encouraging an individual to buy an addition or an upgrade that will make a product more expensive. Think of if your customer wanted to buy a ticket to a movie—you may ask them if they want the VIP seating, knowing that it will up their cost significantly if they do. This is effectively just trying to get someone to pay for the premium version of whatever was purchased initially. It is trying to upgrade something, such as offering more coverage on an insurance policy, knowing it would raise the bill.

Cross-selling is the act of encouraging the purchase of something else if someone is already buying something. For example, if you see that your customer is buying an item, such as a pan, you offer them an item that is frequently bought with that particular one, such as spatulas or cleaning supplies specific to the pan. You are effectively trying to get them to add to their purchase in hopes of getting more revenue. Think of when you're asked if you want to buy something else at a restaurant. "Can I get you anything else? Would you like dessert?" These are attempts to cross-sell.

If you want to be able to properly cross-sell or upsell, you will want to consider the following:

- **Understand the audience:** Make sure that you pay attention to the information about the audience. What is their demographic? What are they buying? How much o they usually spend? This is all important to determine what could possibly be upsold or if they would be interested in cross-selling.
- **Build upon the customer journey:** Wait for the individual to leave a good review and if they do, you can know that they are quite satisfied. You may even start to get referrals from people that they recommended. At that point, when you know that they are satisfied and spreading the word, you know that they are probably going to be interested in upselling or cross-selling.
- **When in contact with the customer, listen actively:** You may be able to cross-sell or upsell during the initial interaction if you are doing it in person. If you are directly interacting with the other party, you can usually begin to work on signals that your customer may want more. You can pay attention to their actual desires and if they mention that they want something that naturally segues into your cross sell or upsell, take advantage of it.

Chapter 3: Segmentation and Content Personalization

At some point, you need to be able to segment up your market. As nice as it is of a sentiment to think that the whole world will be your target audience, is that really the case? When it comes right down to it, trying to market to everyone is going to cause you to lose money. However, what you can do is make sure that you market to a specific target audience.

Defining your target market audience, then, becomes one of the most important aspects of your job in trying to control the situation around you. If you want to control what is going on and be certain that your marketing is effective, you need to make sure that you can define who you want to target in the first place. You need to know exactly who it is that you intend to advertise to. When you know who your target market is, you will be able to ensure that you are using your money to advertise strategically rather than trying to create something that will appeal to all audiences because there is no real way to appeal to everyone.

Within this chapter, we are going to take the time to consider two of the most common ways that you can break up people into target audiences so that you will be able to focus and avoid wasting money on people that probably would be uninterested anyway. Think about it—you could make the cutest little diapers ever, but really, only parents and people who care for young children will ever buy them, no matter how much you market them. While you may get the occasional person who chooses to buy a box because they are getting a gift for a friend that just had kids or they are donating, for the most part, if you want loyal customers, you are probably not going to pay attention to the people that do not have children or are past that child-bearing age. This is not because you are judgmental or anything, but rather because you are focusing on the most likely audience for the product: Parents and caregivers. There is little to be earned setting up advertisements to try to get people to buy your diapers for a donation drive or for a gift when really, the people who make up the bulk of the market for diapers are parents.

We will be looking at that logic within this chapter. We will take a look at both using segmentation and using personalization to try to target specific people so that you can make sure that you are well aware of what they need, meaning that you can further specify your target as well. When it comes down to it, a target market is a group that you can count on to be effective so that you can make sure that your category is specific.

Segmentation

Market segmentation happens when you target your customers based on very specific characteristics so that your marketing campaigns can be more specific and more opportunistic. If you want to be able to figure out who is going to be the best target for your particular product, you can leverage segmentation when you are able to utilize it the right way. As you read through this section, we will take a look at what market segmentation is, why it matters, the four distinct types of segmentation that exist, and how you can effectively create a market segmentation strategy that will help you.

What is market segmentation?

First, let's define what market segmentation is in the first place. Market segmentation is the process through which you are able to divide a target market into several more specific categories. Instead of looking at an entire group of people, for example, you would want to take a look at a specific age or sex. You may even want to break it up further than that as well.

Effectively, segmentation is the way in which you can define and categorize several people into smaller groups to place them with like individuals that are likely to engage in the same sorts of behaviors so that you can be fairly certain that you are focusing on the right demographic.

When it comes right down to it, being able to segment the market is highly important. You want to make sure that you are able to identify the right kind of market so that you will know exactly how to make your money. Think of the example of parents and diapers—you have already broken people down into a category. You have parents and nonparents. However, if you want to break that down even further to sell those diapers, you may want to look at how expensive your brand is and market accordingly. Are they organic, naturally sourced diapers that are supposed to be better for the environment, or are you advertising an affordable option for people that may be in a tight financial position? You can choose specifically who your target is based on financial limitations—if you have those organic diapers, you are probably targeting upper-middle-class families who are on the organic/free-range bandwagon at the moment, and you can charge a bit more successfully. No matter how good your marketing is, there is no way for you to convince people who cannot afford the product to buy it, so marketing toward lower-income people who are already paycheck to paycheck probably will not help you.

Why segment the market?

Now, you may be wondering why we should segment markets in the first place. Surely, you can just get people to buy the items anyway if you do not focus on a specific market, right? The problem is, however, that if you do not make it clear that you are offering a product that those people in that particular target audience has, you are probably not going to get as many sales. People who are uninterested in your product probably will not buy it anyway, so you will want to make sure that you are actively working accordingly. You want to make sure that you are choosing the items that will work best for you, after all. Now, let's look at eight reasons that you should segment your market if you want to be effective:

- **You create a better marketing message:** When you can pinpoint that target audience, you know exactly who you are trying to reach with your messages. This means that you can use direct, specific messaging to the target audience rather than anything else. You can tell your audience exactly what it needs to hear, such as appealing to specific needs and unique desires. For example, if you are marketing those diapers, you may be able to point out that their product is organic and sustainably sourced, appealing to that one niche category.
- **You can market with the most effective tactics:** With the dozens of options out there for marketing, you can make use of the right ones when you use have a target audience. Instead of going for

broad tactics, you can usually work with narrower choices. You will be able to figure out the best marketing methods when you have that specific target audience.

- **You can target your ads:** Instead of working with vague ads, you can focus your ads on the target audience. With those specific characteristics identified in your segmentation, you will be able to create targeted ad campaigns that focus on specific parts of the work.

- **You can attract good; quality leads:** With clear marketing and direct targeting, you are much more likely to get those quality leads—the people who are actually interested in the product. You will be able to bring in ideal prospects that are much more likely to convert into customers.

- **You can set your product apart from others:** When you make it a point to target tactfully, you can set your product apart from the competitors. You will not blend in because you will be able to define specifically how your product will help meet the needs of specific people.

- **You can develop a better relationship with customers:** When you know what it is that your customers want more than anything because you have segmented them, you are able to better provide them with what they want. You will be able to communicate that you are offering them specifically what they are looking for, something that is going to help cultivate the right kind of relationship with them.

- **You can find those niche market opportunities:** When you segment your targets, you are able to look for underserved markets so that you can then develop specifically for them, meaning that you can get a product out there that is going to be more effectively marketable with less competition.

- **You can keep yourself focused:** When you keep your market targeted, you are able to track what you are doing and keep them on task. After all, you would not want to create something only to find that you actually missed the mark entirely because you happened to get distracted. When you segment, you keep your target focused and, therefore, more specific.

Demographic segmentation

When it comes to segmenting your market, you have four primary bases that you can use. Demographic segmentation is just one of them, and it consists of several other subcategories as well. Demographic segmentation in particular, is one of the more popular forms that can be used and typically breaks people down into categories based upon the statistical data surrounding them. There are several different examples of ways that you can segment demographically and all of them have their specific uses at some point or another, regardless of whether you are targeting B2C or B2B audiences. Depending upon what you are marketing, you will probably make use of different segmentations. For example, if you are working with a B2C audience, you will probably make use of categories such as:

- Age
- Gender
- Location
- Income
- Familial/Marital status
- Education
- Race/ethnicity

Notice how all of these categories will tell you something statistically about the person that you are targeting—you are looking at something about who they are, what they do, and you can begin to predict their buying patterns as well. This is entirely statistical and is not taking a look at personality or preferences—it is specifically looking at measurable information.

With a B2B audience, however, you will probably make use of segmentation such as:

- Company size
- Job functions
- Industry

Psychographic segmentation

Psychographic segmentation, then, is the division of an audience based on factors that are related to their personalities and individual characteristics. When you use psychographic market segmentation, you are looking to identify certain kinds of people on the basis of their beliefs or attitudes rather than who they are statistically. This is usually a bit more difficult to identify just due to the fact that beliefs are subjective, and they are not going to be backed by data in the same way that demographics are, but it is just as valid a way to identify a target and reach out to them.

For example, imagine the idea with the organic diapers again. When you are targeting an audience based on psychographic segmentation for those diapers, you would probably want people who value having their children living a life free from unnatural products or chemicals. They are probably the same people who make use of the organic section in the grocery store and are happy to pay extra to know that the items are safe.

Some of the different categories of psychographic segmentation include:

- Personality type or traits
- Attitudes
- Values
- Lifestyles
- Interests
- Psychological influences
- Beliefs, both conscious and subconscious
- Motivators
- Priorities

Behavioral segmentation

Behavioral segmentation involves the segmentation of how a customer is likely to behave. It looks at actions and habits, looking for patterns. You will be analyzing your target audience's actions and how they tend to interact with different brands and services. You will want to then target those typical actions. For example, you would look at the fact that your targeted audience typically buys organic products regardless of the cost, and you would then focus on pushing that point.

Common categories for behavioral segmentation include:

- Spending habits
- Purchasing habits
- Status
- Interactions with other brands

Geographic segmentation

Finally, geographic segmentation is the simplest of all—it segments customers and target audiences simply based upon the geographic location of those particular customers. This is typically done with segmentation such as:

- Country
- City
- ZIP code
- Climate
- Rural or urban living situation

Using market segmentation

When it comes to creating market segmentation, you have several options. You will, however, want to follow these specific steps:

1. **Analyze existing customers:** Figure out what it is that your current audience says, performing an audience analysis. This will require you to learn about the customers that you have so that you can find the trends that will help you figure out that target audience.

2. **Create your buyer persona for the ideal target customer:** Next comes figuring out who your ideal customers are. Figure out the exact type of person that you want to attract to your business. The buyer persona will encompass that person, and you will then be able to figure out how specifically to attract that particular ideal customer to guide your marketing.

3. **Identify market segment opportunities:** When you figure out what the market segment opportunities are, you will be able to identify the ways that you will be able to market. In particular,

you will want to ask yourself several questions here, including:

- What are the problems that your brand can solve?
- What problems will your brand or product solve in a way that is more complete or better than your competitors?
- What does your team serve?

4. **Research:** Next, you must make sure that you research the potential segment that you think that you will utilize. Make sure that you are looking to see what kind of competition you are likely to face, how you can find audiences that are interested in your new market, and more. Figure out everything essential about your ideal target audience and push the point.

5. **Test:** When you have researched, you can then start to explore and test. Try testing out the campaign that you are pushing and see if you are getting the results that you are looking for.

Content Personalization

Alternatively, you can make use of content personalization instead of market segmentation. This is a similar way to address target audiences by recognizing that different visitors are going to visit your websites for different reasons. Some may be first-time visitors, and others may be there regularly and are loyal. While it is standard to use websites that display the same content, no matter who the visitor is, you can start to narrow down what you display for your clients or customers so that they see items or displays that are relevant for them.

You can set up websites that will display content that is specific to the visitor. You can set up calls to action that are specific as well, typically making use of a template that will then tailor the information that is given to the customer based on personal data that you can access. It will help you to tailor your content presentation to the specific visitors to your website so that you can get them to purchase more often than you would if you did not try to target at all. This is done through access to information such as location, search history, and even purchase history if you already have an account with that particular site.

Think about the last time that you went shopping online. Did you have a list of items that were chosen "Just for you" that showed items that are similar to what you have bought in the past? Did the ads that were presented at the top of the page reflect searches that you have done recently? These are ways that you can implement content personalization, and they can be highly effective, depending upon the implementation. Typically, the information that is used and applied includes:

- Age
- Gender
- Location
- A device that you are using
- Frequency with which you visit the site
- The date and time
- The referring URL
- Purchasing history and habits

Think about how some sites will show up completely differently based on the region that you are in. You may look at a site from your iPhone in Seattle with a link from Google, and you will get one version of a site, but someone using their desktop from their location in Canada through a link presented on Facebook may get an entirely different site, specific to their locale.

Personalization is becoming highly popular—in fact, it has been adopted so much that 92% of marketers claim that they use personalization in their strategies in one way or another. There are all sorts of ways that you can personalize content, from making personalized emails to the website or the app that is presented. Only 8% of marketers claim that they do not use any sort of personalization at all.

The most common source for personalization, by far, is email; they will send content that is personalized, either to the purchases, to items that may catch the viewer's eye or any other methods. If you can make use of personalization, then, you can provide your customers with so much that will help them to figure out what to buy, and when you are engaging with your customers in ways that display specifically what you think that they would like, you can usually convince them to buy easier than if they got the default site presented to them. You just have to make sure that you are delivering the right kind of content.

Content personalization by segmentation

Of course, you can combine your personalization with your segmentation to make an even more effective method that you can use to attempt to attract customers. When you use target audiences by segmentation, you can usually provide people with information that will help to sway them. Imagine that you sell watches. Do you want to advertise only female watches to men? Probably not—it would not be a very effective form of marketing, though some men would probably buy as gifts for people they care about. However, if you set up your site so that it can detect whether the user typically purchases men's or women's items, you can then make sure that you display your information accordingly.

You can use any of the forms of segmentation that have been presented to you if you want to personalize—you just have to make sure that your information that is provided is relevant to the viewer. This is great for emails and website experiences so that you can encourage more general engagement, but you are also limited somewhat because you will be targeting a segment rather than an individual.

Persona-based personalization

This type of personalization requires the use of personas to create relevant content for users. It involves creating personas for segments, even if anecdotal, and then begins to market that way. Data is collected about an individual through their browsing history to create a persona for them, which is then targeted. This is ideal when you are marketing based on someone's account history. Imagine that you have a site and have been tracing the engagement of your users. You would generate that in this manner, allowing you to figure out what it is specifically that you will need to do to target your clients.

You may, for example, see that your customer has purchased diapers, baby clothes in several sizes, and has looked at baby furniture. You would then presume that this customer is probably expecting a baby and would market accordingly based on that persona.

Customer journey-based personalization

In terms of creating the best customer relationship, you probably want to consider the customer journey-based personalization. When you use t his, you will be providing content that is relevant to where in the customer journey your customer is. This requires you to make customer journey maps, which will then track the progress of your customers. Your map should provide you with the details that you will need to use to target your customers at different stages. You may offer emails trying to guide someone back to your site after they have abandoned a cart. You may use a post-click landing page to provide a free resource to try to get someone interested in your site. There are all sorts of ways that you can target based on the customer journey, depending upon the products that you are marketing.

Individual-specific personalization

Of all of the personalization methods that you have been offered so far, this is the first that is individual. If you want to make sure that you are targeting individually and without focusing on broader audiences, you want to make use of this form of personalization. It will help you to truly personalize the content that you are providing. The only way that you can do this, however, is to create a highly segmented picture of who your individual is in real-time and then provide the content that was optimized for them. This could take what you know about their spending habits as well as their purchase history and other demographics to provide items that are related to the ones that the person was just looking at, for example. You will need to use AI to manage this—you will be aggregating and analyzing data drawn from your customer in real-time and then having the AI program make decisions to ensure that you are giving content that is highly relevant. You can create one on one emails that will directly address the content that the individual was looking at, or you can create post-click landing pages or special offers specific to that individual.

Choosing the Method that's Right for You

When it comes to making your choices, then you have no shortage of options. One thing is for certain; however—you need some sort of personalization if you want to be successful. Whether you want to market to entire categories of people or if you want to try to market individually, if you want to have that solid relationship with your customers and move them along in their journeys, you will want to make sure that you provide some degree of personalization.

As you can see from this chapter and everything that you have been provided thus far, you can recognize the undeniable benefit that comes from making certain that you provide customized content. People are creatures of habits and when you can break down and understand those habits as well as meet specific needs in certain niches, you can usually get far with trying to market to other people. This is highly effective, and if you want to be able to tap into those habits, you need to make sure that you market effectively.

Think about what you want to do and the resources that you have. Is your particular product or business something that you will need truly individualized marketing for or will you be able to get by with segmentation? Do you have charts for customer journeys so that you know what kinds of emails and offers to send people at different stages in their journeys? Make sure that these are all considerations that you have when trying to set up your marketing plan.

Chapter 4: Customer Value Management

When it comes to figuring out your target audience, you must also be able to assign some sort of value to each customer that you market toward. If you are marketing toward customers that have a higher value, you are more likely to see better returns on the investments that you make. Ultimately, business is business and if you are trying to make money, you will probably want the best potential return on investment that you can get, which means that you have to know which customers are the ones that will provide you with the most potential value for your money. If you want to be successful in managing everything, you will need to make sure that your marketing is in the right place.

You may want to market those diapers that we have been discussing—but to do that, you need to know which segment is going to give you the best return, and ultimately, that return will hinge upon customer value management. Which market is the one that will offer you the best potential value? That is determined entirely by the customer's perception of an item. Someone that does not have babies probably would not value diapers very much at all. To them, they have no reason to buy, and therefore, they have no reason to value those diapers. They do not care about buying baby products that they will never use, and therefore, marketing to that particular demographic is not going to be very beneficial at all. You will want to make sure that you find the demographic that will actually value your product enough to invest in it.

As you read through this chapter, you are going to be introduced to the idea of customer value management—this is being able to manage the customer's view of an item's value. It is not fixed and you can influence it if you know what you are doing. If you want to be able to control the value that others see, however, you will need to understand the intricacies of customer value management in the first place. You will need to understand what it is, why it matters, and how to make use of it. You will need to know how to calculate it out and also how you can begin to influence it. Ultimately, if you can make solid use of CVM, you will be able to make sure that your marketing is effective.

Defining Customer Value Management

Imagine for a moment that you are shopping for a shirt for an interview for work. You go through the racks at your local department store, looking for just the right one. You find the perfect shirt and pull it off the shirt, only to see the price tag. The store is asking for $95 for the shirt. You look it over. It looks right, it fits right, but the price makes you hesitate. You ultimately decide that $95 is too much for a shirt that you will not regularly wear, so you put it back and keep looking, before ultimately choosing out a shirt for $35 that does not fit quite as well or look quite as nice. Why do you choose the lower cost shirt despite the more expensive one looking better?

It all comes down to the perceived value of that shirt. You may like the shirt enough, but you do not value it enough to spend almost $100 on it. You think that it looked great, but not $100 great. After all, for the average consumer, $100 can go a long way. The $35 shirt, while not as nice, is more in line with what you would expect for the price. The value and the price align just right, so you buy it. Why is that?

This is exactly how customer value plays out—when a customer has a specific value set for an item that they are willing to pay, not much will make them buy if that price is over the value. We do not like feeling like we are overpaying, and that internal customer value is one of the ways that we have to help us determine if we are or not. When it comes right down to it, the customer value of an item is our guiding light to purchases.

You may be wondering, then, what this has to do with your own business. Why does it matter what other people think of the value of your product? You, the manufacturer, may value that shirt at those higher amounts, but if the customer does not agree with that sentiment, you will find that your shirt will never sell. You will find that ultimately, people will not care enough and will not bother to buy at those price points. This goes to show that it is not just your own perceived value to an item—you must also consider the value that is perceived by others.

This is where CVM comes into play—it tells you just how much your customers happen to value the products that you are marketing. If you want to measure the perceived value for the money, you need to look at what the customers think. After all, if the customer is king, you want to make sure that you are paying attention to their perceptions as well, especially in a world where there is no shortage of other competitors to your product. There are other shirts out there, as you saw in this example, and people will go with something that they deem as lesser if the price is right compared to the price of your item. This means that, if you hope to develop that proper customer relationship to get the loyal customer base that will keep your company thriving, you need to make sure that you have the right customer value in the first place.

The Benefits of Customer Value Management

When you can align your customer value and the price that you are asking for your product or service, you are able to set up for success. If you have an organization that is selling shirts, you want to make sure that they are priced according to the customer value so that you can actually retain customers. Remember, happy customers are repeat customers, and if you make use of optimizing the CVM along with the product that you are selling, you can raise the retention rate of your customers. This can be done thanks to the wide range of benefits of customer value management that exist. If you want to be able to guarantee that your customers will love your product and be more likely to return to buy more, you must make sure that they are satisfied with the value to price as well. these are just some of the benefits that you can reap if you are able to align your CVM accordingly:

- It is preferred when trying to create accountability for marketing. Because you will be able to look to it to see how people value your product, you can use that measurement as a reflection of the marketing successes that you have had. It also serves as a map to help you market your goals effectively. You can use the CVM as a sort of goal for your marketing, such as deciding that you want to raise the CVM to a certain level.
- It focuses on what customers think, meaning that you will be able to get data-driven ways to improve the ways that your item or product is seen by customers, enhancing the value.

- It is the key to making sure that your business is developing. When you want to ease a product into the market, you will be able to look at the CVM to determine whether the product will be successful or if you should be considering the creation of a newer product. When you use this effectively, you will be able to develop the right kind of marketing, modeling, and strategies that will help your product succeed. Additionally, it can also help you to figure out who to market to and how to start pushing those beneficial relationships with your clients or customers, as well as manage your sales better.
- You can calculate the value by looking at the benefits and how those are valued and then subtracting the costs to see how worth it to your customer it is. This means that you can take a look at just how likely it is that your item or product is going to be used or purchased all by seeing how often it is valued by people in the first place.

Using Customer Value Management

If you want to get started with customer value management, you will want to take a look at how to optimize and understand it. We have already said that the value is roughly calculated out by figuring out the perceived value of an item and then subtracting the costs. This then gets used to figure out how valuable the product was for the customer. Let's go back to the idea of the shirts. That $95 shirt may have been valued at roughly $50 for the individual—they saw the value that they would get out of having that shirt, compared to the average shirt of maybe $35, as being just $50. That is more valuable than any random shirt, but it is also nowhere close to the $95 asking price. Because the value minus the price is -$45 here, the individual is not going to be likely to buy.

They will feel like they wasted money. If they valued that less than ideal shirt at just $35 because it was nothing special, they break even, but in their mind, the value is already $45 better just because of the fact that they are not losing money. If they feel like they overpaid by $45 for that first shirt, feeling like the price is right is going to seem like a much better deal.

There are five steps for customer value management, then, that will help you to ensure that your business is successful. If you can follow these five steps, you can begin to optimize the perceived value that customers have when they look at your object.

Step 1: Discovering what it is that drives the value that your customers perceive

This is done primarily through engagement with your customers. You will need to speak to them and get to understand what they think about your product. If you want to make sure that your product is valued, you need to get out and talk about it. Ask people what they would think about the item that you are selling. Ask them how much they would pay for something like that. Conduct surveys in which you get out and figure out how people respond to your product. The more information that you have about the product, its strengths and weaknesses, and perceived value, the more that you will be able to complete the optimization.

The catch here, however, is that you will want to follow this feedback. You may think that your product is perfect, but if you are not the target audience, your opinion is not really relevant here unless you are only in it for yourself or as a hobby. If you want to make money and run a business, your customer matters more than you do. Your customers' opinions will ultimately be what determine the success that your company has. Follow their advice and their lead.

Step 2: Identify the value proposition, and then implement it

When you have conducted your surveys, it is time to figure out what the value is that your customers perceive. This is done by calculating out the benefits of a product and then subtracting the costs. This will determine how well your product is valued, and of course, this will vary greatly from location to location. In a low cost of living area, you may see that minimum wage, or even average wages, are half of what you would see in a higher cost of living area, and because of that, the perception of the value would vary greatly. In that low cost of living area, paying $100 for that shirt may require 12 or 13 hours of minimum wage work to pay for it, whereas in a higher cost of living area, it would be just 6 or 7. That will skew the value of your product as well.

Figure out during this time just how much your target customers will devote to paying for your service. This will probably be done by looking at what they are willing to pay or seeing what competitors price at in your general area as well. This is highly important to figure out what you are doing with the costs of your product. When you can follow this all, you will guarantee that your work is done effectively.

Step 3: Determine the target audience to get more value compared to competitors

Ultimately, you are constantly in competition with other options that exist within your niche. If you sell diapers, you are fighting against all of the other companies that sell diapers as well. If you sell shirts, you have to make sure that yours are more valuable than many of the others. If you want to be competitive, then you have to undercut those competitors, or at the very least, provide more value relative to the product than your competitors provide and this can be a bit tricky. You need something that sets your product apart and will allow for your product to then be deemed the one that will be chosen over the others.

The perception of your value versus your customers will vary greatly for different people, depending upon all sorts of factors, ranging from location, income, and more. One segment may find that your product looks amazing, while others want nothing to do with it, and that is highly important to recognize and remember. If you want to make sure that your product is purchased, you will want to make sure that you understand how it is seen compared to those competitors.

Step 4: Create a price point that works for both sides

From there, you will want to figure out what the right price point is for your product. If you want to get the best customer value rating from that particular product, you need to figure out that point in which you still profit, but your customers still find that they are getting value. Keep in mind that even just pricing your product at low values will not be enough to work long-term. Remember, people will have no problems with rejecting even low-cost items if they are not getting the right value. However, satisfied customers, those who actually enjoy the products that you are offering, will find that they get much more value out of your product. This means that you must constantly be managing that fine line between a product that is fantastic to use and a product that is going to give you the right value. If you can do this, you will find that you will be much more successful. Make sure that you are satisfied with the profit and that your customer is satisfied with the value. When you reach that point, you will find that everyone wins.

Step 5: Invest on the best customers

One point to consider is the value of the individual customers that you have. If you are going to be selling products, you need to make sure that you are investing in those customers that are going to give you the most bang for your buck. You must make sure that the value that you are getting is effective. When you can do that, you will find that you are getting much more value than you otherwise would. This means that you should absolutely be prioritizing being able to get those customer returns by figuring out which segment is going to benefit you the most.

When you can figure out which segments are the most valuable to your business, you can then make sure that you address those segments in particular. You will be able to work to make sure that you put out products that will be well-received by those clients, which will help you to make sure that you continue to attract those characters.

Calculating Customer Value

Customer value, then, is the driving factor of your entire campaign. If you want to market effectively, you must make sure that you know what the value your product has. It is perhaps one of the most important values of the entire process—when you understand the true customer value; you can help yourself figure out just how much money that you can spend on customer acquisition. After all, you would not want to pay more in acquisition than your product is valued at; otherwise, you are losing money instead of gaining. When you can understand your value, you can then make sure that your customers are satisfied by making sure that you give them a better value for their money. The better you can set up the value compared to the cost of your product, the more likely you are to get that customer retention.

Measuring customer value is highly important, then, and it is not nearly as difficult as you may think. You are not working with concrete numbers here—you are simply figuring out a ballpark estimate for the value of the product that you are offering, and then you compare that to the price that you want to ask.

Just remember this equation:

Sale price- Cost of Goods = Customer value

If you can keep this in mind, you will be able to compare the value of your item to that of your competitors to make sure that you can always keep that edge somehow.

Customer value is typically calculated out during a specific period of time to see if your product or business is actually valued. You will set a specific time period, such as a 1 week period. You then want to calculate the average order value during that period of time.

When you want to calculate the average order value, you will need to use the following calculation:

Average order value = Revenue total during the 1-week period/ Number of orders over 1 week period

Imagine that you sold 15 orders of shirts over that 1 week period of time and made $600.

Your average order value, then, must be calculated out with the following equation:

600/15= 40

This tells you that your average order was worth $40.

You then want to consider the purchase frequency of your product. This is the number of times that someone will buy from you during a period of time. You should still be working with the same period of time from calculating out the average order value. In this case, you are going to need the following equation:
Purchasing frequency = Number of orders during a 7 day period/ unique customers during a 7 day period

When you calculate this out, then, you may say that the 15 shirts were bought by 10 different people, and you get the following:

15/10=1.5

This then tells you that each of your 10 customers buys an average of 1.5 shirts during the week.

Now, you can calculate customer value. To do this, you will want to take the average order value and multiply it by the purchase frequency. In this case, you get the following:

40/1.6=25

This tells you that your average customer is worth roughly $25 per week. This is how much they value your business as well—after all, if they did not see that your product was worth that amount, they would not have been willing to purchase. They would not have given you the business that you have gotten if they did not see your product as worth that.

Changing Customer Value

Customers value all sorts of aspects of their products. Some value the convenience of a product, which is why going out to restaurants usually costs so much more compared to buying the food and cooking it yourself—you are paying for the convenience and the cost of creating that product. Some value is earned by the quality of the ingredients. If you want to increase the perceived customer value so that you can price your product higher and still retain those sales, you have a few ways that you can do exactly that.

Time matters

We value time more than money and for a very good reason—time is finite whereas you can always earn more money. If you want to make sure that you are getting the money that you want or need, you need to make sure that you are valuing your product accordingly. If you can make it clear that your product saves time, you can make it more valuable.

Convenience

Of course, you can see that time is valuable, specifically in looking at convenience. The more convenient something is, the more valuable it tends to be as a direct result. If you want to save money, you are probably choosing the less convenient option. The reason convenience tends to cost more is because assembly or preparations still had to be done—but you are paying to have that done by someone else. Consumers will usually buy products if they believe that they will be more convenient. Someone who is very busy one evening may prefer to pay to get takeout for dinner because it is simpler than taking the time to cook when time is already scarce.

Conscious capitalism

This is the idea that what you are doing is befitting something else. Think of how many products these days market that they will donate a certain amount of their profits to a charity—this is good for everyone. Most customers would prioritize a product that is going to be donating money, and they would switch to a charitable brand if the price were comparable. However, 20% of consumers report that they will go out of their way to buy a more expensive product if they feel like the cause is worth supporting. This means that philanthropy sells- it is worth the perceived value and can actually increase the value of a product.

Locality

Locally sourced or locally made items also are perceived to be credible and, therefore more valuable. These are more common than ever, and when you source local ingredients, you are supporting your own community and your own environment as well. There is not as much mobility, which means that there are fewer trucks shipping items. There is less packaging and items go from production to shelves quicker because they are local. This means that, for you, selling in your local area may be easier and more valuable than selling and shipping online.

To create more value for your item, then you would want to market one of the points that were listed above. If you do that, you can make your product seem more valuable, meaning that you can raise the prices and still come out ahead. If you are producing products that are believed to be valued in these ways, you can continue to sell while upping the price.

If you want to do this, you will need to go through trial and error. You will need to take the time to figure out what it is that your customers want and how you can interact with them. You will need to make sure that you are pushing what you know that you are working with your clients and customers as opposed to against them.

Chapter 5: Analytics and Performance Measurement

When it comes right down to it, you need to be able to measure the performance of your CRM so that you can tell whether or not you are being effective with the tactics that you are using. You want to make sure that you are actually working with your products and making sure that your attempt to increase relationships with customers is working well. To do this, you need to understand how to measure the performance of that CRM so that you can analyze your success. There are many different ways that you can analyze your CRM approach's performance, and in this chapter, we are going to look at several.

Remember, CRM encompasses just about every single part of your business. It encompasses everything that you do, from how you interact with the people that you are trying to entice to buy from you to the people that you employ. There are many ways that you can increase your performances and tell just how effective your business is, such as using any of the methods that you will see here.

Within this chapter, we are going to consider both how you can measure that particular metric, as well as how you can optimize it to ensure that you are using the best possible CRM strategy that you can.

Customer Retention

Customer retention matters greatly—when you have higher customer retention, you know that your customers are successful. When it comes to knowing if your company is doing a good job, knowing that you have a good retention rate is one of the easiest ways to find out. If you have customers coming back, they are clearly satisfied with the product or service. After all, would you go to a subpar restaurant that you hated and then decide to go back again the next time that you went out? Most people do not want to feel like they are wasting money and if they are disappointed with the service that they got from a product, they are going to feel like they have wasted money, especially if they go back again in the future.

Acquiring customers is expensive—it usually costs far more to acquire that first customer than it does to keep them around, and because of that, you want to make sure that you are doing your best to invest in the customers that you have. When it comes down to it, you want to make sure that the customers that come back are the ones that you prioritize. Customer retention should be one of the most important points that you emphasize in your CRM.

If you notice that your customer retention is low, you will want to determine what you can do to retain those longer-term relationships. Reach out for feedback. Figure out what it is that is making people change their minds with their expectations and what they are doing. Figure out how you can keep up with the ways that you engage with your customers. Ask for them to tell you why they have left if they have, or ask for reviews for customers that come back again and again. When you do this, you can get information about what you can do better, and you can also increase retention with making sure that you have the value just right as well as making sure that you offer coupons and discounts or send emails with deals and recommendations for other items that they can use. Make sure that you have a marketing funnel set up so that you can work on retention as well.

Visits and Orders per Customer

For CRMs that are performing well, you can usually see that they are bringing in plenty of traffic. The well-performing CRM will also have people that visit increasing. If you want to measure how well your CRM is doing, then, you want to consider just how much your visits and orders have increased. If you see that your visit and order statistics are actually decreasing, there could be a bigger problem at hand as well.

The best thing that you can see is that your visits and orders are going up instead of down or staying the same. If you realize that your visits and orders are not increasing, it is time to consider why—there is probably a reason for it that you will be able to find if you try to do so. If your numbers are not changing, it is time to consider if you can advertise better or if you can market to a different target audience. There are all sorts of ways in which you can increase the way that you interact with your customers so that you will be able to increase those numbers, and typically, marketing is the right answer.

Sales

Similarly, you can tell how your CRM is doing by looking at the sales. If your product is not making a profit, your product is failing. You cannot run a company without profit, and without sales, profits are impossible to make. This means that you need to make sure that you are selling, preferably increasing sales constantly. You want to make sure that you are able to increase the sales that are made, either in increasing the number of orders that are placed or in increasing the average spending at any given point in time. You want to work on getting your customers to buy more products or to get more customers to come and purchase as well.

When you want to better your CRM, you must make sure that you increase the average spent per customer or the number of sales that you have. This is usually done through intensive marketing that is designed to help push the products that you have to offer. Maybe you work to make sure that people see your product and want to purchase it. Maybe you work to ensure that you email often or you have popups reminding people to buy more. Maybe your sales teams are trained better to close on those deals, or you offer a discount if people refer others to you. No matter the methods that you choose, however, if you can up your sales, you can usually improve upon the CRM as well.

Cross-Sells and Up-Sells

Cross-sells and upsells are two ways that you can work to see how well your CRM is doing. Generally speaking, both cross-sells and upsells will increase if you are working well and if your CRM is effective. Remember, cross-sales involve you selling other products on the same site—you may have drawn someone in to get just one item, and they buy two or three. Upselling involves getting people to go for a more expensive product instead of the lower-cost option, typically in the form of upgrades to the product.

When you want to increase these, you need to ensure that your customers see your products as valuable in the first place. This may involve having some deals every now and then or making use of targeted marketing to show why your customer actually does need that extra product as well because it will serve them well. Commonly, on websites, you will see this done through the use of lists of items that are frequently purchased alongside the item that you are about to buy, showing people that there are other options as well that may be highly useful to them that they should also be considering alongside the one that they are there to purchase.

When you work hard and start to increase both upsales and cross-sales, you know that you are working to improve your CRM as well, and that means that you are on the right track to success with your company.

Renewal Rates

Renewal rates are quite important to pay attention to—you want to make sure that your customers, if applicable, will renew subscriptions or service agreements. For example, perhaps you are marketing a cleaning service subscription. For a flat rate, you offer one cleanup session per week, plus one big deep clean every 6 weeks. If you have people renewing their subscriptions for your services after the first period ends, you know that you have customers that are satisfied with your company. This is great—it means that you can trust that your customers are getting something that they value, and they are willing to continue paying for that value.

If you notice that you are not getting those renewals, however, you may find that your customers are unhappy. This could be a problem with the product or service itself, or it could be an issue with the management or the people involved. After all, even if you love a product, if you find that the individual people that you have to interact with are less than pleasant, you probably will not really want to renew that service. People tend to be people-oriented and if relationships are not pleasant, people will often take their money elsewhere—they want to be appreciated and treated with respect.

If you find that those renewals are not happening, you want to double-check the ways that you are interacting with the clients and customers that you have. Are they friendly interactions? Are they usually filled with mistakes being made? Make sure that you are serving your clients and customers with the right attitude to get them satisfied with the products that you are providing. If you can do that, you will likely see those rates go up.

Sales Calls

Sales calls that are made out are those that will go out between customers and the sales representatives in hopes of making a sale. This is typically done by contacting people who have been in contact with your company in the past and attempting to sell them on buying something else from you. It is usually prearranged and is oftentimes, even face-to-face. Think of the interactions that you may have with a car salesperson or an insurance agent—they are trying to sell you a product, but they are only trying to sell those products after you approach them about being interested in the first place.

You want to make sure that you are able to make more sales calls. When you are able to make more sales calls, you are usually able to increase your profits as well. The increase in sales calls will directly correlate with a successful CRM—if you are doing a good job with the entire business, you are likely to see that your clients are willing to come back to you time and again and that means that you will naturally see an increase in those sales calls, especially if referrals also happen and if your marketing calls are successful.

If you notice that your numbers are suffering, however, you may want to consider implementing other options as well. You may want to work on that advertising or working on getting the word out that you are open and available to get those customers interested.

Winback strategies

Winback refers to customers that were unhappy with something but then came back. Think about it—it is impossible for every company to always deliver exactly what the people want. It is impossible to always keep everyone satisfied and because of that, you must also make sure that you are working to ensure that your customers' problems are handled effectively.

Think about a time that you had a bad dish at a restaurant and decided that you did not ever want to go back there again. If they, upon hearing of your dissatisfaction, decided that they would offer a discount or a replacement meal to try to get you to buy from them again, and you were satisfied, you would be considered a winback. You are someone that was unhappy with a product, but then liked how it was handled so much that you decided that yes, you would go through with patronizing there again in the future.

This is perhaps one of the greatest ways to win loyal customers—when people know that your business will help them if they are unsatisfied about something, they are much more likely to be willing to purchase, especially if they feel like for the most part, your products are absolutely worth buying. Most people are reasonable and understand that, sometimes, things go wrong and that it is necessary for things to get fixed after the fact.

Of course, this means that you must have a solid way planned to help your clients if they are unhappy. Ask yourself what you can do for them if they ever are unhappy— what can you offer them that will help them remain satisfied? Are you going to offer a generous return period? Do you offer discounts for problems? Do you want to do whatever you can to satisfy your customers? When you make sure that you do this and you do it effectively, you know that your CRM is functioning properly.

Referrals

We all love referrals—when we get referrals, we know that someone was satisfied with our products enough to recommend them to someone else. With customers that you have impressed and retained, you also get the benefit of referrals as well if you know what you are doing. One customer has a lot of power—they can share their happiness on social media for all of their contacts to view, for example. They can tell their friends about how great your product or service was if they hear from their friend that they are looking for one.

Referrals are essentially free advertising. If you want to make sure that your product is getting the attention it deserves, you want it to have enough wow factor to make people feel compelled to share it in the first place. If you can do that, you can usually influence all sorts of people into helping or buying from you.

If you find that you are regularly getting referrals at higher rates with the implementation of a CRM, you are probably on the right track to what you are doing, and you are probably going to want to continue doing what you are doing. If you are not getting referrals, however, you are probably not pleasing your customers enough to ensure that they are all satisfied.

Revenue per Salesperson

The amount of revenue per salesperson tells you just how well each of your employees is doing in regards to sales. You want to make sure that people are getting great rates for sales so that you know that they are going to be effective. Make sure that you are paying attention to the ways in which your customers are able to make their sales. Are they getting higher close rates or are they struggling to get people to move from that prospect to a customer?

Sales tactics are important—you must make sure that your salespeople know what they are doing and that they are armed with everything that they will need to ensure that they are able to close. This means that you will probably want to track customer journeys and make use of marketing funnel strategies if you are still struggling to get that revenue per salesperson numbers up, but if you can do that, you will usually find that you are actually able to begin boosting those struggling numbers to ensure that everyone is satisfied.

When it comes right down to it, having competent salespeople is often incredibly important. If you notice that you have struggling salespeople and revenues are not where they should be, you may need to figure out some training to help to boost those scores. However, if you see those rates increasing, there is a good chance that your CRM is thriving. After all, customers will not buy if they do not think that it is worth it.

Marketing Return on Investment

The return on investment that is made is incredibly important. If your ROI is negative, you are simply not going to be able to sustain the investment—it is losing money, and that is a problem. Losing money means that you are doing something wrong somewhere. It could be that your product or business model is simply not profitable. It could be that you are targeting the wrong audience with the wrong tools. You may even find that there are other problems going on elsewhere with training or quality.

If you realize that your ROI is not growing, or is too low to sustain yourself, you can work with your CRM to ensure that you can optimize it. You can work to figure out everything that you need to do to make sure that your products are highly capable of being successful. You want to make sure that your product is going to return profits to you and that sometimes means creating a brand new strategy for yourself.

When you use CRM properly, you can usually increase the returns that you get from your marketing investment. However, when you see the ROI start to drop, you know that there is a major problem. It may be that you have seasonal slumps—after all, if you sell in-ground swimming pools, you probably do not have much of a market autumn through spring. However, it could also be that there is a disconnect somewhere that needs to be addressed. Begin analyzing your target audience again to make sure that you are aiming in the right place to figure out how to keep your clients around.

Customer Lifetime Value

Customer lifetime value is a prediction model that will tell the general profit that is believed to be generated for a relationship with one customer. It is effectively the monetary value of the relationship between consumer and company for however long that relationship is maintained. This is a highly important value—you want higher CLV because you want to make sure that your customers are satisfied. Usually, satisfied and loyal customers will naturally have higher and better CLVs than those that are not. Again, it is far cheaper, in the long run, to pay to keep your customer happy than it is to have to get a new customer. It always pays to build up that loyalty before having to build up new people to work with.

CRM Metrics

When it comes to the specific metrics for CRM, typically, you will be taking a look at eight key points—organizational performance, customers, processes, infrastructure, IT, human capital, strategic alignment, and culture.

Organizational performance

This refers to the measurements of diagnostic factors—they will give you information about the performance of your CRM approach. IN particular, you will see three key parts to this metric:

- **Shareholder value:** This refers to the value seen for the shareholders.
- **Profitability:** This determines the perception of performance to figure out just how profitable the particular business is and how it is doing. You will

usually see this as being highly related to ROA, ROI, and net sales.

- **Customer equity:** This is typically subjectively measured through what is perceived to be the loyalty rate and then through looking at how often customers tend to return. It also has to do with the customer lifetime value as well as profitability rates.

Customer

This particular metric looks at how the customer is going to view the particular organization to tell just how much value the customer puts on it. You want to know how many people that will use the item value it so that you can tell whether or not it is effective or if there are changes to be made. Typically, customer engagement and customers that enjoy the program are signs that a CRM is working as intended. The tools that are usually used here include:

- **Customer loyalty:** This is related to the perceived loyalty of the customers to tell how likely it is that your product is valued.
- **Customer retention:** This is related to the retention rate for customers—it is effectively customer satisfaction and the rate of customers that are satisfied with the product as delivered for people.
- **Customer value:** This is the subjective measurement of the perceived value of the brand that you are marketing, as well as the relationship between customer and company.

Process

Process refers to diagnostic factors that will determine how well your business model is designed. It is meant to look specifically at how your customer strategy is doing to make sure that it is all in line and working as intended. It includes:

- **Customer acquisition:** The subjective measurement of telling how many customers are being acquired, as well as how they are acquired. It includes measurements such as response rate, the rate at which customers are contacted, the lead per channel, the visits to a website, the profitability of new customers, and the rate of sale.
- **Customer retention:** This is the rate at which customers are kept and willing to continue business with your company. In particular, you will look at how often you have clients return, how many problems that you resolve, whether your customers are satisfied with the resolution, and the customer churn rate.
- **Customer expansion:** This refers to the readiness that customers have to expand and grow—it refers to the number of people that are willing to be encouraged through up sales and cross-sales.

Infrastructure

Infrastructure is primarily focused on looking at four key points, which will then be addressed in depth within the rest of this chapter: IT, human capital, strategic alignment, and culture. Each of these will have their own specific diagnostic factors, much like all of the other factors that we have looked at so far.

IT

IT typically makes use of CRM technology—the measurements of subjectivity include being able to look at the quality fo information that you have, as well as how usable the entire system is. It takes a look, effectively, at everything that you can do within the business to keep it working smoothly. If it has to do with technology, websites, or anything else, it is monitored here. In particular, it focuses on accuracy, customer information, and system stability.

Human capital

Of course, you cannot have a business without people, and because of that, it becomes imperative to look at the behaviors of people as well. They are valid and necessary parts of any business at this point in time and because of that, CRMs have ways to measure how well their people are working at their jobs. This is effectively going to manage the people that work there.

- **Employee behavior:** This measures how employees interact with their customers and the attitude that they take when they are interacting with someone. They include as well the tangible tools of looking at human capital readiness to look at the training that goes into the people that your company employs, as well as the time spent on each particular job.
- **Employee satisfaction:** This refers to the ability to tell how satisfied employees are. After all, you want to make sure that your employees are happy with their jobs so that they will do the best possible job at the end of the day. If you want your employees to be as happy as possible, you will work with them to ensure that they are comfortable in the workplace. You can identify this through the turnover rate that you can identify with employees. Companies with high turnover rates usually are struggling.

- **Management attitude:** This refers to the idea that the CRM is being supported by the management of the company. Effectively, you are looking at how many people readily accept the system that is being used and whether the management is working to ensure that it is all implemented successfully so that the employees can follow along easily.

Strategic alignment

Next comes taking a look at the strategic alignment of a group. This involves making sure that the strategies being implemented behind the scenes are put together properly so that it is possible for the employees, and therefore the entire company, to be set up for success. A successful alignment is there so that your company will work well and smoothly. It includes tools such as:

- **Training:** This refers to the training that goes into the employees to make sure that everyone has all of the necessary knowledge to help their customers or to do their jobs effectively. Without training, it is impossible to make sure that jobs are done effectively. Typically, you can measure this directly by taking a look at how often you host training to keep everyone up to speed and working effectively.
- **Organizational structure:** This refers to the flexibility that a tool has with the organization. Is it able to keep running if there is a snag hit somewhere, or will the entire system come grinding to a halt? Your company should have some sort of resilience somewhere and somehow to be effective. With this particular measurement, you will be taking a look at just how diverse your organization is—is there any redundancy? How can you get rid of it to keep everything running smoothly?

- **Reward system:** This refers to the rewards that are given to an organization to determine to keep everyone working together in tandem. You can measure this specifically by looking at system usage—how much of your system serves a purpose? How many of the employees are working hard to follow along with everything as well? These are important points to consider.

Culture

Finally, culture must be considered as well. This is all about the attitudes that are taken within your company, and for the most part, they will be driven by the people that work there and permeate everywhere through the interactions that you have. If you want to have an effective culture, you must make sure that everyone is on the same page and working efficiently together. It includes metrics such as:

- **Partnership:** This refers to just how much coordination there is between people or departments. You want to make sure that you have strong partnerships build in your system so that it will all work functionally and smoothly. In particular, you will look at vendor diversity to determine how well your partnerships are going. How many external companies or vendors do you have? This is an important consideration to make.
- **Market orientation:** This refers to the measurement of the orientation of the market. It typically means that you are looking at how often your customers engage with information that could be useful to you. In particular, you are going to want to take a look at how often your customers will complete customer surveys.
- **Explicit goals:** Finally, you need to have goals that are explicit. These are highly important to ensure that everyone is working together toward the same end goals so that you can be certain that everyone will be on the same page and work toward the same end.

When you want to measure your CRM, you will be looking at all of these points. You will be asking yourself if you are hitting those points and making sure that if you are not, you are taking steps to repair the problems in the first place. When you can do that, you can increase sales and therefore fix just about every problem that you otherwise would have suffered.

CRM is a highly effective tool if you can implement it the right way, but it does take time and effort, as well as plenty of trial and error. If you want to be effective, you will need to be mindful of this and make sure that you keep that in consideration. If you are able to remain diligent and dedicated, you should find that you are actually able to begin to improve your business, no matter how it was doing prior.

Conclusion

And with that, we reach the end of this book. As you read, you were introduced to the idea of Customer Relationship Management, and for very good reason. The number one takeaway from this book is that it is far cheaper to maintain your current customer base than it is to try to find a new one. Acquisition of customers is expensive and time-consuming, which ultimately only translates to even more out of pocket costs. When you are able to manage your relationships with your customers effectively, you know that you are making a move toward doing what is right and what you need to get done. If you can keep up with everything that you need to do, you can often find that you are able to succeed with your business and customer relationships just by treating your customers with respect. Value your customers. Remember that, without them, you would not have your business at all. They are valuable—they have to be if you are competing against all sorts of other products just to get your hands on their money. Business is not personal—people take their business to the best place they can, driven by perceived value more than the cost of something. It is not always enough to set your prices underneath your competitors if the product itself is subpar.

Your customer's matter and the sooner that you accept and recognize that, the sooner that you will be doing well with the business that you have. You must remember that at all times, you are doing what is right for them. Business is all about making sure that both your business and your customer are benefitting—it should be symbiotic in nature rather than anything else and if you can make sure that that is the case, you can usually ensure that you are able to keep your business afloat as well. It may not be easy at times, but it is something that you can do effectively if you know what you are doing.

As this book comes to a close, remember that you were given some key information as you read. You learned all about why digital Customer Relationship Management matters now more than ever. It is highly important for you to remember that you must make use of these strategies in the most effective ways possible so that you can be successful with your endeavors. If you want to make sure that you are working with your clients in ways that will make them come back again and again, you have to know what you are doing and how to set up with CRM in the first place.

Remember that you have no shortage of strategies that you can use digitally to help generate those leads that will serve your business well. From understanding what the customer's journey looks like to being able to create those leads that you will need, you will be able to succeed if you can implement the right kinds of strategies. In particular, in this book, we focused on digital strategies to really emphasize the ways that you can directly interact with your clients and your customers digitally. Digital media is becoming king in this world, and that means that we have a duty to adapt and comply with that digital nature. It is imperative that ultimately when you do interact with those around you, you focus on how best to navigate with your clients and customers. Focus on methods such as email marketing, push notifications, and SMS to really get people interested. You can direct mail people or even engage in all sorts of onsite activities that will help to keep your clients interested and engaged in what you are doing so that they will come back time and again.

Recognize that sometimes, it is far better to only target one specific group of people for your sales than it is to try to reach more people. It is next to impossible to put out a product that will truly apply to every single person. Even basic products like toilet paper have non-toilet paper alternatives. We are surrounded by competition, so rather than trying to become the next big thing for everyone, it is more important for you to focus on attracting that target audience to what you are doing. When you do that, you can make sure that you are working effectively so that you can be certain that you get more sales. Think about it, would you rather have that subpar ad that no one really cares about or the one that really appeals to the group of people that you want to sell to? Segmentation and personalization matter immensely these days, especially when you are competing against so many different products out there on the market. You are not alone, no matter how clever you may think that your product is, and you will need to rely on your marketing abilities to prove that you will be able to live up to those standards and win those sales and support.

You will also need to keep in mind that customer value is going to rule everything about your success. You must make sure that at the end of the day, your product is valuable to the customer and the best way to make that the case is through the use of customer value management. You can work to adjust the ways that the people around you see your product, and in doing so, you can typically work to raise that value up with tactics such as philanthropy, which most people will naturally pay more for just on principle alone. People like to help other people, after all, and even better, philanthropy is typically tax-deductible as well in many places, meaning that it benefits you to donate anyhow.

Finally, it becomes imperative for you to consider the performance of your particular CRM to make sure that it is working effectively, and because of that, you will want to always make sure that you are going over points such as rates of renewal or calls. You want to ensure that your performance measures appropriately for the CRMs that you are running, and you want to ensure that ultimately, you are able to keep up with everything.

If you can keep these points in mind, you can start working on setting up your own CRM system. Remember, there are several points to it. You may decide that you want to utilize the software on your computer to help with it. You may decide that you want to train your employees in certain practices to help with your performance. You may decide that you will work on changing your marketing practices. There are very few limitations to how you must proceed—so long as you are keeping in mind that the value that your customers bring in is worth struggling to retain those customers in the first place and that it is highly important for you to make sure that the clients that you have were satisfied.

Thank you for taking the time to get through this book, and hopefully, as you did read it, you found that the information that you were provided was highly useful and beneficial to you. Hopefully, as you read, you found that being able to see what matters the most behind the scenes really does matter immensely and that you are able to begin making the right changes to ensure that you and your business are successful.

From here, all that is left to do is start implementing the processes that you are adding! You want to make sure that you plan out your attack, and you figure out exactly what it is that you will need to do to ensure that your business can get that CRM up and running sooner rather than later. Do not forget just how lucrative that doing so can become and just how effective it can be to make sure that the people that you are working with are satisfied—both employees and customers.

Thank you once more for making it this far, and if you found that this book has been particularly useful to you, please consider heading over to Amazon to leave a review. It would be greatly appreciated and highly desired! Good luck on those future endeavors getting that CRM set up, and don't forget—a little bit of perseverance always goes a long way! All you have to do is make sure that you do not give up once you get started.

Printed in Great Britain
by Amazon

15687370R00062